SUPERMAN
SCIENCE

OUTRUNNING BULLETS
SUPERMAN™ AND THE SCIENCE OF SPEED

BY *TAMMY ENZ*

SUPERMAN CREATED BY
JERRY SIEGEL
AND **JOE SHUSTER**
BY SPECIAL ARRANGEMENT
WITH THE JERRY SIEGEL FAMILY

CAPSTONE PRESS
a capstone imprint

DC
COMICS™

Published by Capstone Press in 2016
A Capstone Imprint
1710 Roe Crest Drive
North Mankato, Minnesota 56003
www.mycapstone.com

STAR36202

Library of Congress Cataloging-in-Publication Data
Names: Enz, Tammy, author.
Title: Outrunning bullets : Superman and the science of speed / by Tammy Enz.
Description: North Mankato, Minnesota : Capstone Press, 2016. | 2016 |
    Series: DC super heroes. Superman science | Audience: Ages 9–12. |
    Audience: Grade 3 to grade 6. | Includes bibliographical references and index.
Identifiers: LCCN 2016002663| ISBN 9781515709152 (library binding) | ISBN
    9781515709190 (paperback) | ISBN 9781515709237 (ebook pdf)
Subjects: LCSH: Speed—Juvenile literature. | Kinematics—Juvenile
    literature. | Superman (Fictitious character)—Juvenile literature.
Classification: LCC QC137.52 .E59 2016 | DDC 531.112—dc23
LC record available at http://lccn.loc.gov/2016002663

Summary: Explores the real-world science and engineering related to Superman's
super-speed.

Editorial Credits
Editor: Christopher Harbo
Designer: Bob Lentz
Production Specialist: Tori Abraham
Media Researcher: Eric Gohl

Photo Credits
Dreamstime: Chrisstanley, 9; DVIDS: NASA, 11, 26; NASA: 15 (all), 17 (bottom), 27, 28, 29,
Bill Ingalls, 17 (top), DFRC/X-43A Development Team, 13; Shutterstock: Andre Coetzer,
21, Aphelleon, 7 (top), Artyom Anikeev, 19 (bottom), ChameleonsEye, 8, Digital Storm,
19 (top), Fotokostic, 7 (bottom), Gui Jun Peng, cover, Janossy Gergely, 20 (bottom), Jochen
Kost, 14, Jonathan C Photography, 20 (top), Kaliva, 25 (bottom), MCarter, 22, MO_SES
Premium, 16, Solis Images, 18, Steve Byland, 23, SVSimagery, 12, Waldemarus, 10
(speaker); Wikimedia: Axion23, 24, Bri Ham, 25 (top)

Printed in the United States of America in North Mankato, Minnesota.
009667F16

TABLE OF CONTENTS

THE NEED FOR SPEED

Superman didn't become the World's Greatest Super Hero by waiting for crime to come to him. Wherever super-villains lurk, the Man of Steel taps into his power of speed to track them down. Whether outrunning bullets or flying around the globe, Superman always manages to save the day just in the nick of time.

Superman's speed may be out-of-this-world, but Earth has its own examples of speed that might give the Man of Steel a run for his money. For instance, did you know a hummingbird is considered the world's fastest animal? Or that engineers have developed a rocket car that can break the speed of sound? Want to know more? Take a deep breath and hold on tight. You're about to explore the science behind a world with a need for speed.

FACT:

Superman made his first appearance in *Action Comics* #1 in 1938.

WHAT IS SPEED?

For heroes like Superman, speed is essential to staying one step ahead of criminals. In the scientific world, there's more to speed than getting somewhere in a hurry. But what, exactly, is speed, and how does it affect us every day?

SPEED ESSENTIALS

To scientists, speed is how fast an object is moving. It is a measure of the distance traveled in a certain time. Although speed is often associated with "fastness," any moving object has speed. A tortoise inching along has speed, just not as much as a rocket blasting into space.

While defining speed is simple, perceiving it isn't always straightforward. Superman is famous for traveling faster than a speeding bullet, which is about 1,700 miles (2,735 kilometers) per hour. But right now—even standing still—you are traveling faster.

A person standing near Earth's equator spins about 1,040 miles (1,670 km) per hour around Earth's axis. At the same time, Earth whips around the Sun at 67,000 miles (107,800 km) per hour. That's not all. Our solar system hurtles around the center of the Milky Way galaxy at about 490,000 miles (788,580 km) per hour. Now that's fast!

Earth orbits the Sun at the breakneck speed of 67,000 miles (107,800 km) per hour.

STOPPING A BULLET

A speeding bullet only packs a punch when it makes an impact. To stop bullets in the real world, soldiers and police officers use Kevlar. This fabric's strong, tight weave stretches to rob bullets of their energy. Kevlar is the life-saving material used in bulletproof vests.

POLICE

ACCELERATION

Superman can go from standing still to a blue blur in the blink of an eye. This awesome ability to speed up is called **acceleration**. Acceleration is the change in the **velocity** of a moving object. Imagine riding in a car on a highway. As long as the car maintains a constant speed, you don't feel like you are moving. But if the car suddenly speeds up, brakes, or turns a corner, you feel it. That's acceleration.

Roller coaster riders feel acceleration as they zoom down a hill.

One of the best places to feel acceleration at work is an amusement park. The thrill of roller coasters is in their rapid accelerations. The stomach-dropping feeling you get when a roller coaster plummets down a hill comes from acceleration. As you rapidly speed up, you feel the acceleration. When you squash your buddy while rounding a curve, you feel acceleration because your body changes direction. Even the sudden stop at the end of the ride is a form of acceleration called deceleration.

THE WORLD'S FASTEST ROLLER COASTER

Ferrari World in the United Arab Emirates is home to the world's fastest roller coaster. Formula Rossa maxes out at 149 miles (240 km) per hour. This speedy coaster accelerates from zero to 62 miles (100 km) per hour in just two seconds.

acceleration—rate of change of the velocity of a moving object

velocity—a measurement of both the speed and direction an object is moving

ULTIMATE SPEED

In the super hero world, you'd do well to round out your track team with Superman and The Flash. Between the two, no one is faster. In our world, you'd definitely want sound and light on your team. Check out the amazing speeds of these two forms of energy.

SPEED OF SOUND

Sometimes Superman flies so fast he becomes supersonic! Supersonic means faster than the speed of sound. Sound is a wave of **vibrations** that pass through air **particles**. Starting at a source, vibrations pass from particle to particle until they reach your ear. These vibrations move through the air at the incredible speed of 761 miles (1,225 km) per hour. That's like running the length of almost four football fields in one second.

While sound travels fast, its speed is not beyond human reach. Traveling at or beyond the speed of sound is measured in Mach numbers. A vehicle that reaches Mach 1 is traveling at the speed of sound. At Mach 2, it travels twice the speed of sound. At Mach 3, three times, and so on.

The Bell X-1 was the first aircraft to break the speed of sound. On October 14, 1947, Bell X-1 launched from the bomb bay of a Boeing B-29. It then used a rocket engine to go supersonic. Today, most military fighter jets reach speeds of Mach 2 to Mach 3.

Bell X-1

FACT:

On October 15, 1997, the rocket car Thrust SSC became the first car to break the speed of sound. It topped 763 miles (1,228 km) per hour.

vibration—a fast movement back and forth

particle—a tiny piece of something

SONIC BOOMS

One big drawback to supersonic flight is the sonic boom caused when jets pass the speed of sound. A sonic boom is a loud rumble caused when air **molecules** are rapidly pushed aside. It is heard and felt by people on the ground when a supersonic plane flies overhead. It can be loud enough to damage people's eardrums and break windows. As a result, supersonic flight is banned over many countries.

An F-18 Super Hornet creates a vapor cone as it nears the speed of sound.

An artist's rendition of NASA's X-43A hypersonic jet in flight.

While engineers study ways to reduce sonic booms, the race is on to develop **hypersonic** planes that fly even faster. To be called hypersonic, an aircraft must reach Mach 5. On November 16, 2004, NASA's X-43A hypersonic jet set the world record as the fastest aircraft. The unmanned aircraft clocked a speed of nearly 7,000 miles (11,265 km) per hour. That's Mach 9.6!

BOOM!

SUPERSONIC PERSON

Can a human reach supersonic speeds without an aircraft? Felix Baumgartner did it. He jumped from 24 miles (39 km) above New Mexico on October 14, 2012. On his way down he broke the sound barrier, causing a sonic boom. His maximum speed was 834 miles (1,340 km) per hour.

molecule—the atoms making up the smallest unit of a substance

hypersonic—a speed greater than Mach 5

SPEED OF LIGHT

If the speed of sound is incredible, the speed of light is mind-blowing. Light travels at 186,000 miles (300,000 km) per second. At this speed it could circle the Earth's equator seven and a half times in just one second.

In fact, the speed of light is so fast we use it to measure huge distances in space. One light year is the distance a light beam can travel in one year. How far is that? About 6 trillion miles (9 trillion km)! If you think the Moon and Sun are really far away, think again. The Moon is only about 1.3 light seconds from Earth. The Sun is about 8.3 light minutes away.

1.3 LIGHT SECONDS AWAY

8.3 LIGHT MINUTES AWAY

Light travels from the Sun to Earth in about 8 minutes and 19 seconds.

The next nearest star to Earth, Proxima Centuri, is 4.24 light years away. When we see Proxima Centuri, we don't see it as it looks now. We see it as it looked more than four years ago. High-powered telescopes, such as the Hubble Space Telescope, help us see stars millions of light years away. But Hubble actually looks back in time. It sees stars as they looked millions of years ago. Some may have burned out before we even discover them.

The Hubble Space Telescope orbits high above Earth's atmosphere, allowing it to see deep into space.

JUNO SPACECRAFT

No human invention has come close to achieving light speed. But NASA's *Juno* spacecraft, launched in 2011, will soon become the fastest human invention. When it orbits Jupiter in 2016 its speed will be about 46 miles (74 km) per second. That's fast, but still just 1/4,000th the speed of light.

ENEMIES OF SPEED

Just as Superman battles the super-villains of Metropolis, speed has some enemies of its own to overcome. Gravity and friction slow things down.

GRAVITY

What goes up, including Superman, must come down. Gravity is the force that pulls everything toward Earth. You see gravity in action when you throw a ball. No matter how high or fast you throw, eventually the ball returns to the ground.

If gravity's pull is so strong, how do planes and rockets overcome it? An airplane's wings create **lift** to fight gravity. The shape and angle of the wing deflects air downward, creating a push that lifts the plane upward. The faster an airplane travels, the more lift it creates.

Rockets create **thrust** to combat gravity. To break away from Earth's atmosphere a rocket must attain a thrust of 25,000 miles (40,230 km) per hour. Massive amounts of burning fuel spew gases that push off Earth to thrust the rocket into space.

An Atlas V rocket uses the downward thrust of gases to launch toward space.

MICROGRAVITY

As the *International Space Station* circles Earth, it's constantly falling toward the planet. So why doesn't it hit the ground? Because its speed of 17,500 miles (28,000 km) per hour matches Earth's curve. Inside the station, astronauts feel very little gravity because they are in constant free fall.

lift—the upward force that causes an object to rise in the air

thrust—the force that pushes a vehicle forward

FRICTION

Friction's force always opposes motion. Superman battles it to travel fast. But he also needs it to walk or climb stairs. Friction happens whenever two things rub against each other. Rough surfaces cause more friction, smooth surfaces less. You can keep your balance walking across carpet. Walking on ice is trickier because there is less friction.

Pro athletes can't afford to let friction slow them down. Swimmers wear swimming caps to reduce **drag** from their hair. Many also shave their bodies to limit friction with water. Bicyclists shave their legs to fight friction caused by air resistance. Smooth legs help shave time off cyclists' races.

Competitive swimmers wear caps and shave their arms and legs to reduce friction in the water.

SLICK

Slicks give Formula One race cars extra grip on the road.

While athletes try to reduce friction, race car drivers crave it. Racers use tires called racing slicks. These tires may be smooth, but they create more friction than tires with treads. Since more of the tire touches the track, its grip is greater. The extra friction steals some speed from the car. But the slick's grip holds the car to the road on tight corners.

HOT BRAKES

Brakes on cars and airplanes use friction to reduce speed. This friction generates heat. Airplane brakes can reach temperatures of more than 1,800 degrees Fahrenheit (1,000 degrees Celsius). They must be cooled down before they can be used again.

drag—the force that resists the motion of an object moving through the air or water

SPEED IN NATURE

Superman isn't the only being on Earth with the ability to reach incredible speeds. When it comes to the animal kingdom, he has a little competition.

RAPID LAND ANIMALS

If Superman is looking for a competitor in a foot race, a cheetah might be up for the challenge. Cheetahs are Earth's fastest land animals. A cheetah can accelerate from zero to 60 miles (97 km) per hour in just three seconds. With its amazing speed, it knocks down its prey before attempting a kill.

cheetah

FACT:

The sloth is the world's slowest animal with a top speed of 0.15 mile (0.24 km) per hour. It's so slow that algae grows on its fur.

The cheetah would win a foot race against any animal on Earth, including humans. But speed in the animal world isn't just about how quickly creatures move their legs. In fact, some speedsters have no legs at all. Australia's death adder is one of the fastest striking snakes in the world. It strikes, injects venom, and returns to strike position in under 0.15 second. Without **antivenin**, 60 percent of its strikes to humans are deadly.

death adder

FAST FLIERS

When Metropolis' citizens see Superman in flight, they sometimes mistake him for a bird. It's no wonder. Birds are fast fliers. In fact, the peregrine falcon is the fastest flier in the animal kingdom. When swooping to catch its prey, it travels up to 200 miles (322 km) per hour.

Next to the peregrine falcon, the diving speed of the Anna's hummingbird seems slow. It only reaches speeds of up to 60 miles (97 km) per hour during its dives. But this tiny flier actually moves 385 body lengths in one second, which makes it the fastest animal on Earth. By comparison, the peregrine falcon only moves 200 body lengths per second.

peregrine falcon

Anna's hummingbird

Even more amazing are the **g-force** stunts the Anna's hummingbird performs. G-force is the force felt by a body due to gravity. Standing still we feel 1g—or gravity's normal pull. But on a speeding roller coaster, we feel greater g-forces when we're pushed against our seats. In fact, the world's fastest roller coaster produces 1.7g's. And astronauts blasting into space often feel g-forces up to 8g's. But pulling up from a dive, the Anna's hummingbird experiences 10g's!

Mosquitoes aren't fast fliers, but they have speedy wings. They beat their wings 500 times per second.

g-force—the force of gravity on a moving object

HUMAN SPEED

Nature does its best to rival Superman's power of speed. But humans are drawn to that power too. Whether sprinting on foot or zipping around in high-tech machines, people are always looking for the fastest way to get from here to there.

AMAZING AUTOMOBILES

Superman doesn't need a car to speed him from place to place. But humans are always testing how fast they can travel on four wheels. These days, the fastest cars that can legally take to the highway are called supercars. The current supercar champion is the Hennessey Venom GT. On February 14, 2014, it accelerated from zero to 200 miles (322 km) per hour in just 20.3 seconds. At 270 miles (435 km) per hour, it edged out the Bugatti Veyron Super Sport's previous record by just 2 miles (3 km) per hour.

Hennessey Venom GT

While supercars command the highways, jet dragsters rule off-road. Jet powered dragsters are the fastest cars on Earth. One of the earliest jet dragsters was the Green Monster. It used a J-79 jet engine and axles from a 1947 Ford and a 1937 Lincoln. The Green Monster set three land speed records between 1964 and 1965. Its best speed was 577 miles (928 km) per hour set on November 7, 1965.

The Green Monster on display at the Bornemouth Airfield in England in 1968.

WORLD'S FASTEST HUMAN

Jamaica's Usain Bolt is considered the fastest human in the world. The track star has broken the men's 100-meter world record three times. His fastest time, 9.58 seconds set in 2009, remains unbroken today. At top running speed, Bolt flies down the track at nearly 28 miles (45 km) per hour.

EXTRAORDINARY AIRCRAFT

Land speed records are impressive. But when humans really want to crank up the speed, they mimic Superman by taking to the skies. In fact, the SR-71 Blackbird has a lot in common with the Man of Steel. It's sleek, powerful, and can outrun a bullet. The SR-71's speed record of 2,193 miles (3,529 km) per hour, set back in 1976, remains unbroken by any manned jet aircraft. During its 24-year career with the U.S. Air Force, no SR-71 was ever shot down. It flew so high and so fast that enemy missiles never threatened it.

SR-71 Blackbird

North American X-15

Although not a jet plane, the experimental rocket aircraft, North American X-15, actually clocked a speed more than two times faster than the SR-71. At 4,520 miles (7,270 km) per hour, it holds the title as the fastest manned rocket plane. The X-15 was launched from the wing of a B-52 bomber. Each of its flights lasted only about 10 minutes. But they provided engineers with valuable information about aircraft performance at high altitudes and hypersonic speeds. X-15's successes laid the foundation for future space flight.

FACT:

Air resistance made the SR-71's cockpit windows so hot that pilots held their meals to the glass to cook them.

SPEEDY SPACECRAFT

The fastest inventions are those headed out of this world. Escaping Earth's atmosphere and traveling to the ends of the solar system requires maximum speed. To break away from Earth, a spacecraft must travel 25,000 miles (40,000 km) per hour. This speed is called escape velocity.

Usually spacecraft speed is measured relative to the Sun instead of Earth. NASA's *New Horizons* holds the title of the spacecraft with the fastest launch speed. It launched in 2006 with a velocity of 100,000 miles (161,000 km) per hour. In 2015, it reached Pluto and continued onward to explore a region known as the Kuiper Belt.

An artist's rendition of the *New Horizons* spacecraft's encounter with Pluto.

The *Helios I* and *II* solar probes hold the title of the fastest objects engineered by humans. Launched in 1974 and 1976, these probes entered orbits around the Sun. The Sun's mass caused them to reach orbital speeds of more than 150,000 miles (241,000 km) per hour.

The *Helios* probes will not hold their title much longer. NASA's *Juno* spacecraft is expected to reach speeds of more than 160,000 miles (257,500 km) per hour in 2016. In 2018, a new NASA spacecraft, *Solar Probe Plus*, will be launched. Its orbital speeds around the Sun will be 450,000 miles (724,200 km) per hour.

Engineers work on the *Helios II* solar probe prior to launch in the 1970s.

CONCLUSION

Almost nothing slows down the Man of Steel. He can outrun bullets and outfly aircraft. And while his abilities are beyond our grasp, they still remind us that speed impacts our lives every single day. From roller coasters and fighter jets to rocket cars and spacecraft, the science of speed is all around us.

GLOSSARY

acceleration (ak-sel-uh-RAY-shuhn)—rate of change of the velocity of a moving object

antivenin (an-tee-VE-nuhn)—a medicine that helps the body fight off the effects of animal venom

drag (DRAG)—the force that resists the motion of an object moving through the air

g-force (JEE FORSS)—the force of gravity on a moving object

hypersonic (hye-pur-SON-ik)—a speed greater than Mach 5

lift (LIFT)—the upward force that causes an object to rise in the air

molecule (MOL-uh-kyool)—the atoms making up the smallest unit of a substance

particle (PAR-tuh-kuhl)—a tiny piece of something

thrust (THRUHST)—the force that pushes a vehicle forward

velocity (vuh-LOSS-uh-tee)—a measurement of both the speed and direction an object is moving

vibration (vye-BRAY-shuhn)—a fast movement back and forth

READ MORE

Gregson, Agatha. *Fast and Formidable Animals*. Ultimate Animal Defenses. New York: Gareth Stevens Publishing, 2017.

Kenney, Karen Latchana. *The Science of Car Racing*. The Science of Speed. North Mankato, MN.: Capstone Press, 2014.

Peterson, Kristen. *Understanding the Laws of Motion*. Mastering Physics. New York: Cavendish Square Publishing, 2015.

INTERNET SITES

FactHound offers a safe, fun way to find Internet sites related to this book. All of the sites on FactHound have been researched by our staff.

Here's all you do:

Visit *www.facthound.com*

Type in this code: 9781515709152

INDEX